ROMY BERGMANN

HOW to DRAW FOR KIDS

19,440 COMBOS for ULTIMATE FUN

THE SILLY **DRAWING GAME** WITH STEP-BY-STEP INSTRUCTIONS FOR CREATING UNIQUE ANIMALS, KAWAII AND FOODS

Get ready for a silly drawing game packed with fun!

Welcome to the fun and imaginative world of drawing! This book encourages you to dive into an exciting adventure where you can learn to sketch the cutest animals and objects while enjoying endless crazy fun with wild combinations. Mix and match different animal traits to invent new, hilarious creatures with just one roll of a dice!

How to use the book:

Step 1: A Quick Look at the Characters
In this step, you'll discover the unique characters you'll be sketching. Each animal has its own special traits that will inspire you to create fun combinations. These steps are already synced with the dice rounds, so you can practice to prepare for the game!

Step 2: Drawing Instructions
Alright, let's dive in! In this step, you'll find the drawing instructions for each character. We've also thrown in some extra details for the finished picture, which you can add at the end. You can color the finished drawing if you like.

Step 3: Hilarious Mixes
These little sneak peeks give you a taste of the funny and wild things that can occur when you blend the various characters. Get inspired and get ready for the creative chaos that's coming your way in the game!

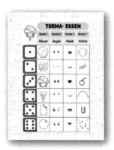

Step 4: The Game
Now we get to the best part - the game! You'll roll the dice over four rounds and sketch what you rolled. Once everyone has finished the first round, we move on to the next. After the bodies, you'll roll for the eyes, the mouths, and the extras.

Tips and tricks for your creative journey!

Drawing tips for the fourth round of the dice game:

Get creative and have fun with your drawings! Place things where they might not usually go—just let your imagination take over! You don't need to replicate all the details exactly as they appear. Do it your way and enjoy the whole creative journey!

Adjust items:

Ears and tail angle adjusted

Omitting items:

lower half omitted

Add items:

Fin was doubled for extra symmetry.

Tips for Sketching and Coloring

Begin with a gentle pencil line: Start by sketching lightly with a fine pencil to outline the basic form of your subject. This approach allows you to make adjustments easily without damaging the drawing.

After you've rolled out all the elements, you can go ahead and trace the outlines with a thicker line. Then, you get the chance to color in your figure and add your own personal flair!

TOPIC: WEATHER

Step 1

Step 2

Step 3

Step 4

Step 1

Step 2

Step 3

Step 4

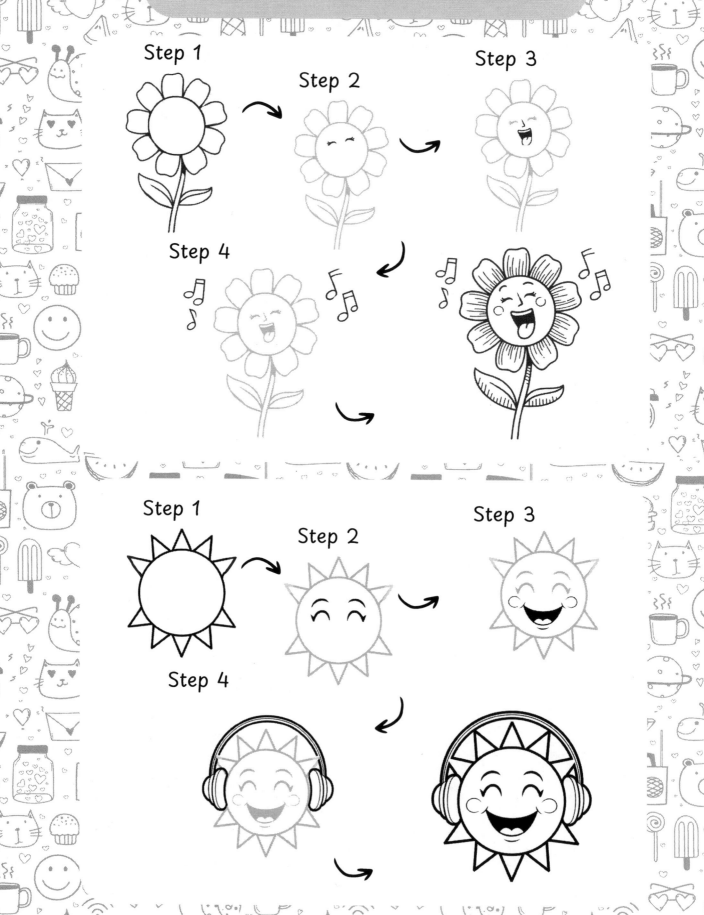

Step 1

Step 2

Step 3

Step 4

Step 1

Step 2

Step 3

Step 4

TOPIC: WEATHER

Step 1

Step 2

Step 3

Step 4

Step 1

Step 2

Step 3

Step 4

ROLL THE DICE AND BE SURPRISED

Here are a few silly combinations

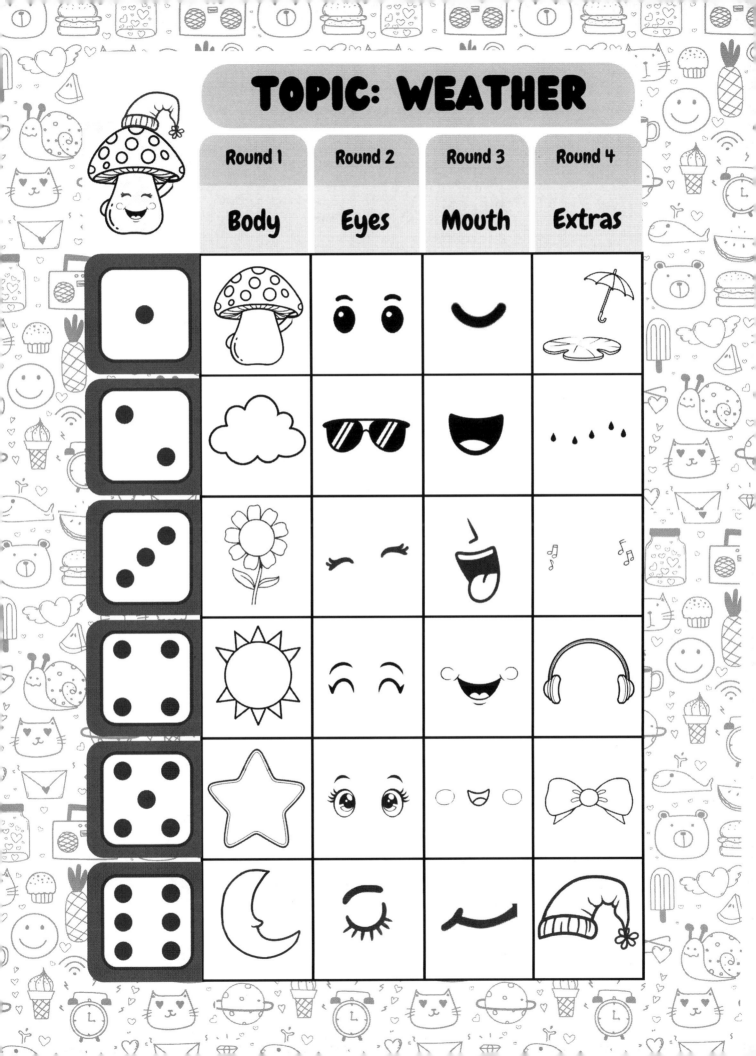

TOPIC: FOOD

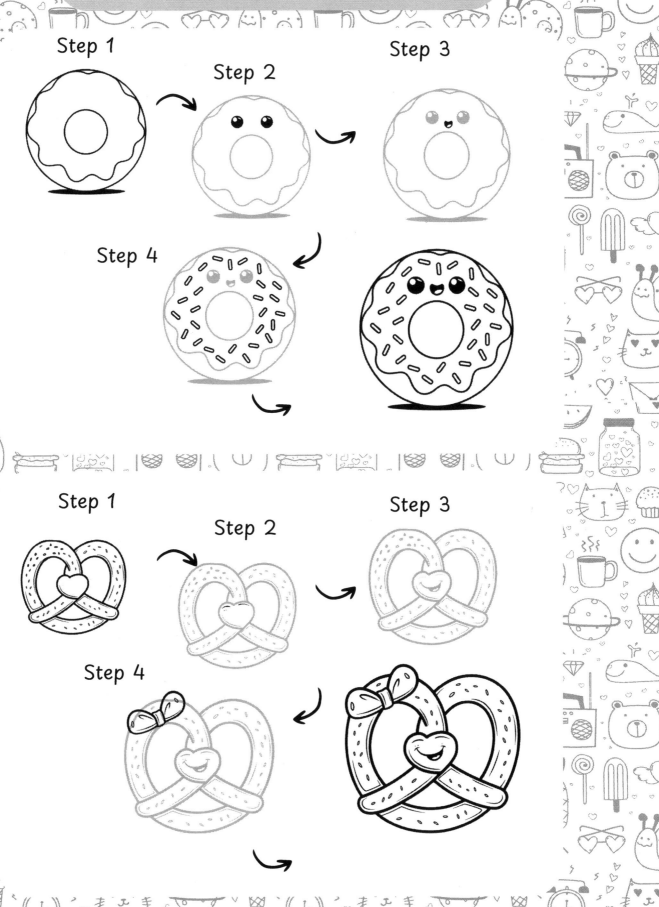

Step 1

Step 2

Step 3

Step 4

Step 1

Step 2

Step 3

Step 4

TOPIC: FOOD

Step 1

Step 2

Step 3

Step 4

Step 1

Step 2

Step 3

Step 4

TOPIC: FOOD

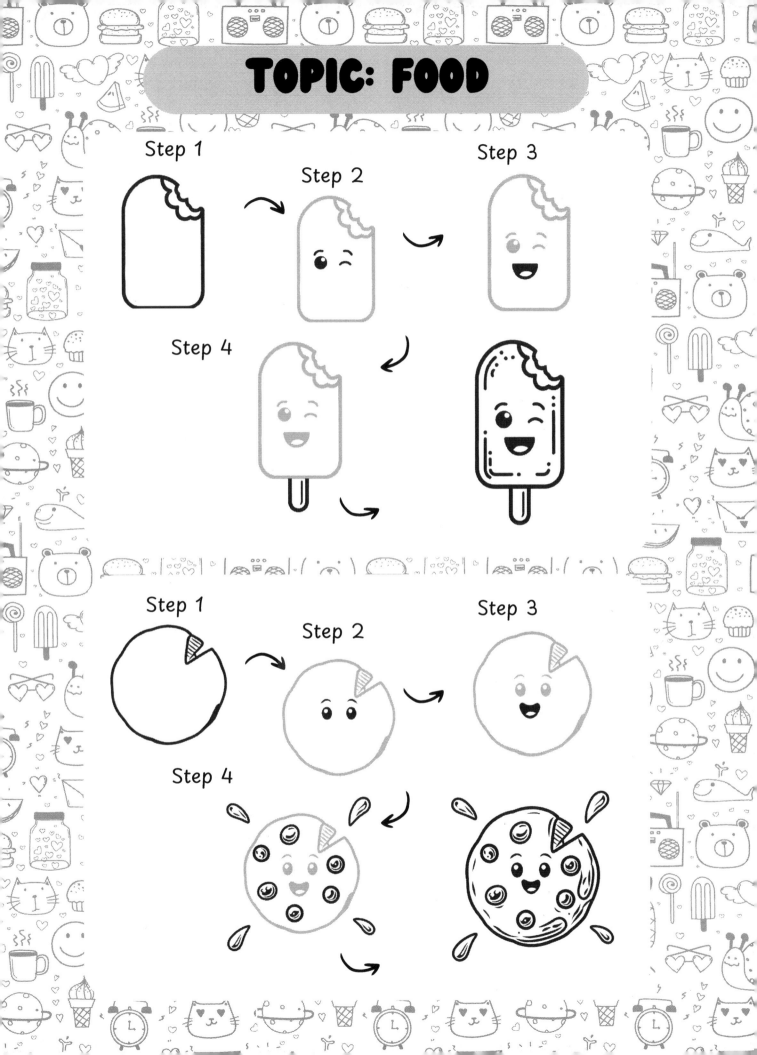

Step 1

Step 2

Step 3

Step 4

Step 1

Step 2

Step 3

Step 4

ROLL THE DICE AND BE SURPRISED

Here are a few silly combinations

TOPIC: FOOD

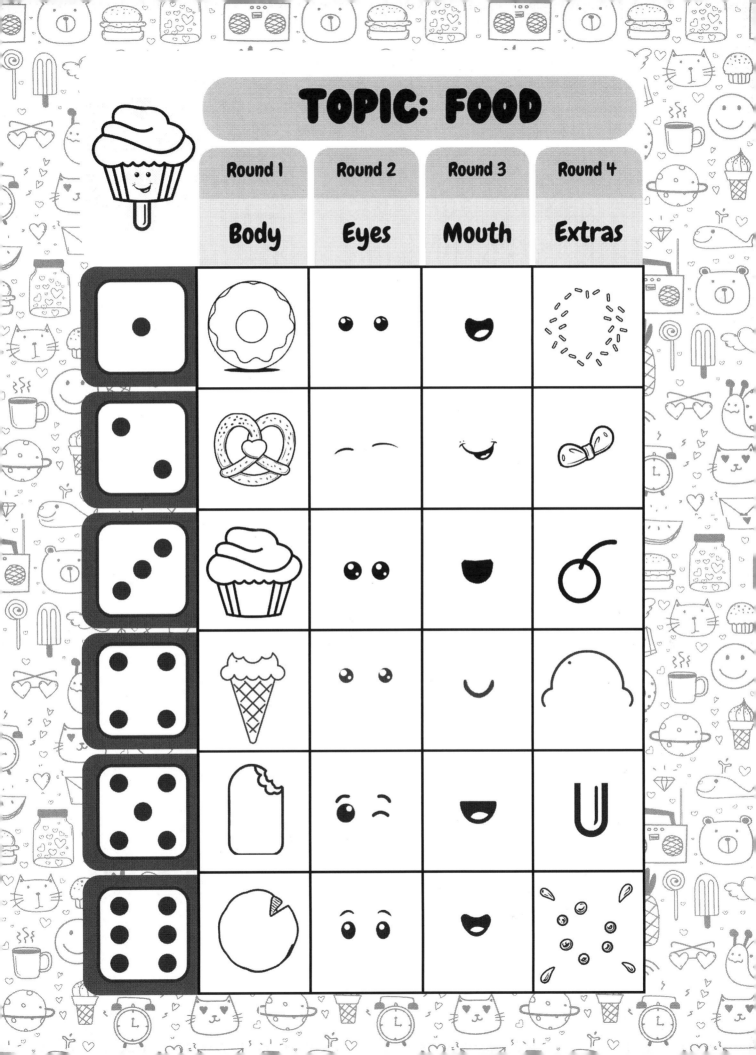

	Round 1 **Body**	Round 2 **Eyes**	Round 3 **Mouth**	Round 4 **Extras**
⚀	donut	eyes	mouth	sprinkles
⚁	pretzel	eyes	mouth	bow
⚂	cupcake	eyes	mouth	cherry
⚃	ice cream cone	eyes	mouth	cream swirl
⚄	popsicle	eyes	mouth	U shape
⚅	cookie	eyes	mouth	crumbs

Step 1

Step 2

Step 3

Step 4

Step 1

Step 2

Step 3

Step 4

TOPIC: FOREST ANIMALS

Step 1

Step 2

Step 3

Step 4

Step 1

Step 2

Step 3

Step 4

TOPIC: FOREST ANIMALS

Step 1

Step 2

Step 3

Step 4

Step 1

Step 2

Step 3

Step 4

ROLL THE DICE AND BE SURPRISED

Here are a few silly combinations

TOPIC: FOREST ANIMALS

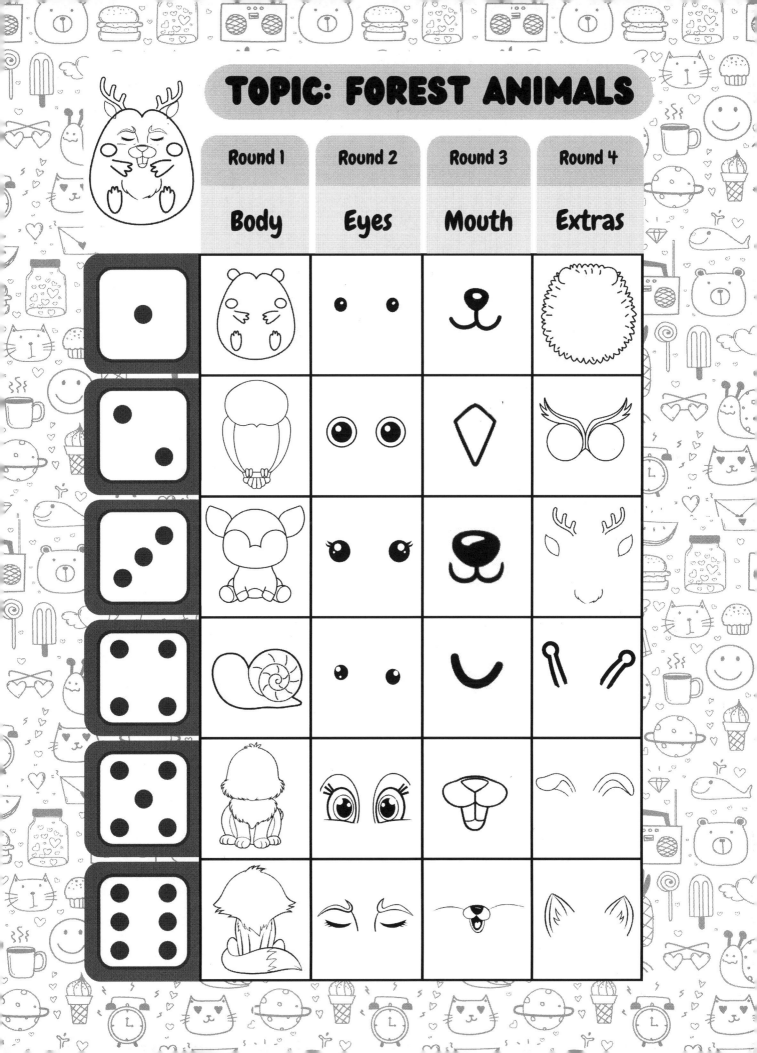

TOPIC: MONSTER

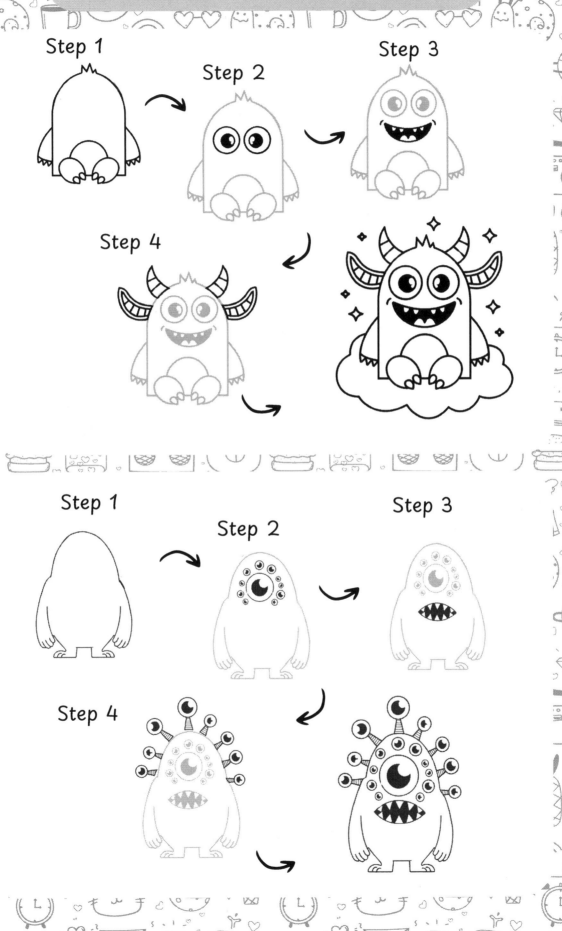

Step 1

Step 2

Step 3

Step 4

Step 1

Step 2

Step 3

Step 4

TOPIC: MONSTER

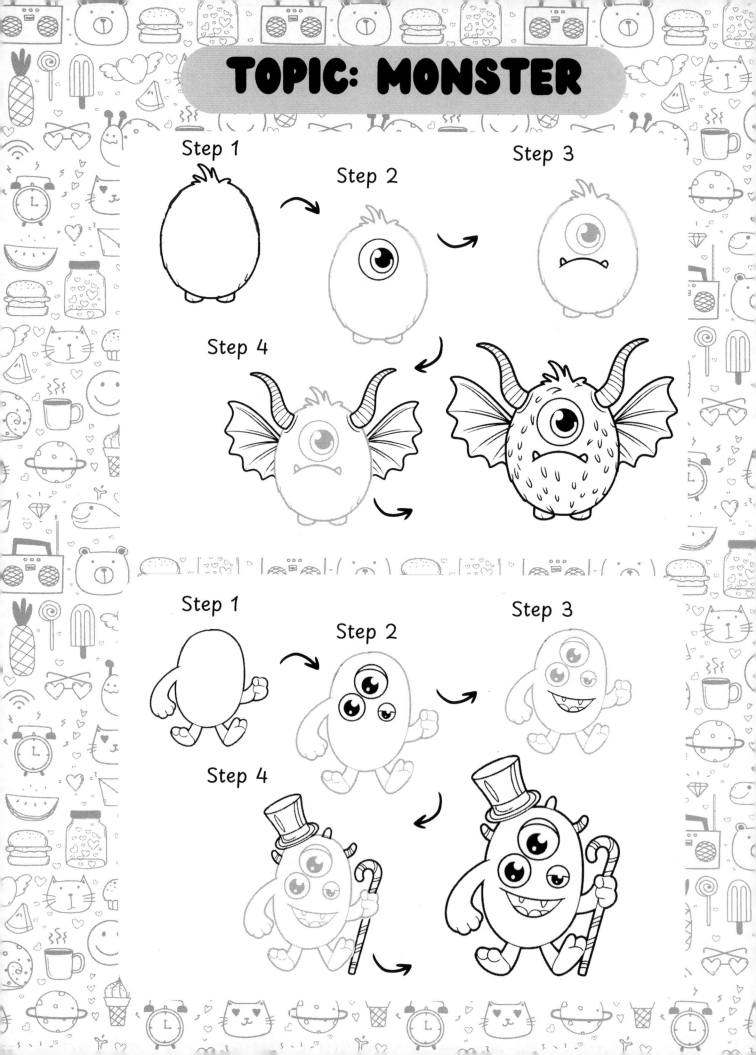

Step 1

Step 2

Step 3

Step 4

Step 1

Step 2

Step 3

Step 4

TOPIC: MONSTER

Step 1

Step 2

Step 3

Step 4

Step 1

Step 2

Step 3

Step 4

ROLL THE DICE AND BE SURPRISED

Here are a few silly combinations

TOPIC: MONSTER

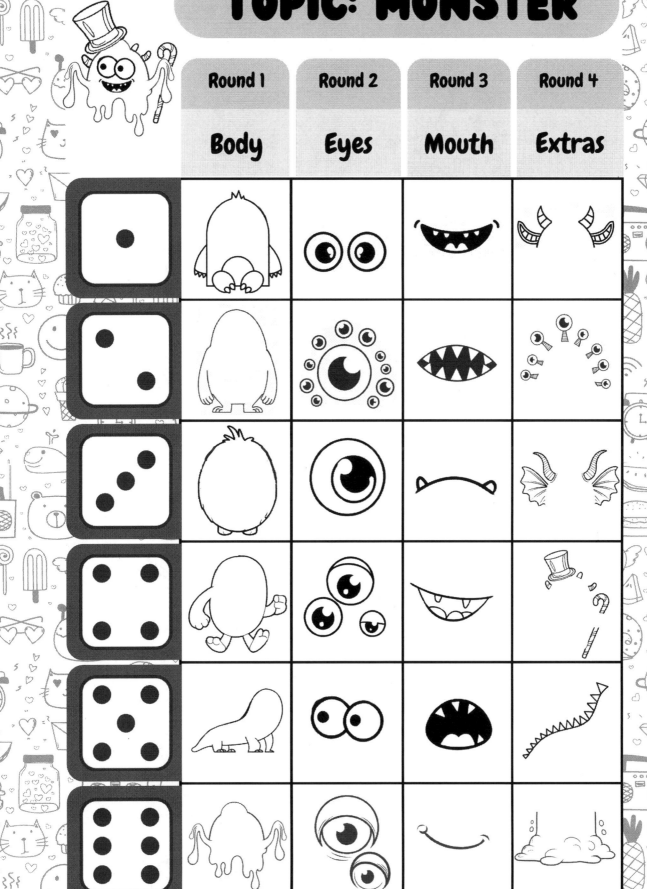

	Round 1 Body	Round 2 Eyes	Round 3 Mouth	Round 4 Extras

TOPIC: SUMMER

Step 1 Step 2 Step 3

Step 4

Step 1 Step 2 Step 3

Step 4

TOPIC: SUMMER

TOPIC: SUMMER

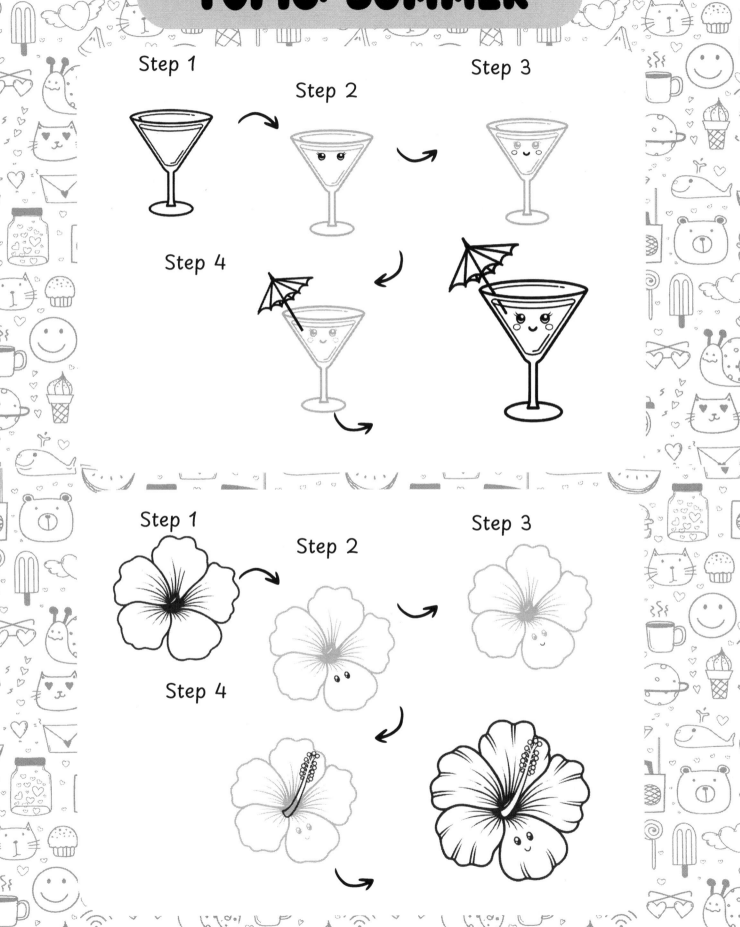

ROLL THE DICE AND BE SURPRISED

Here are a few silly combinations

TOPIC: SUMMER

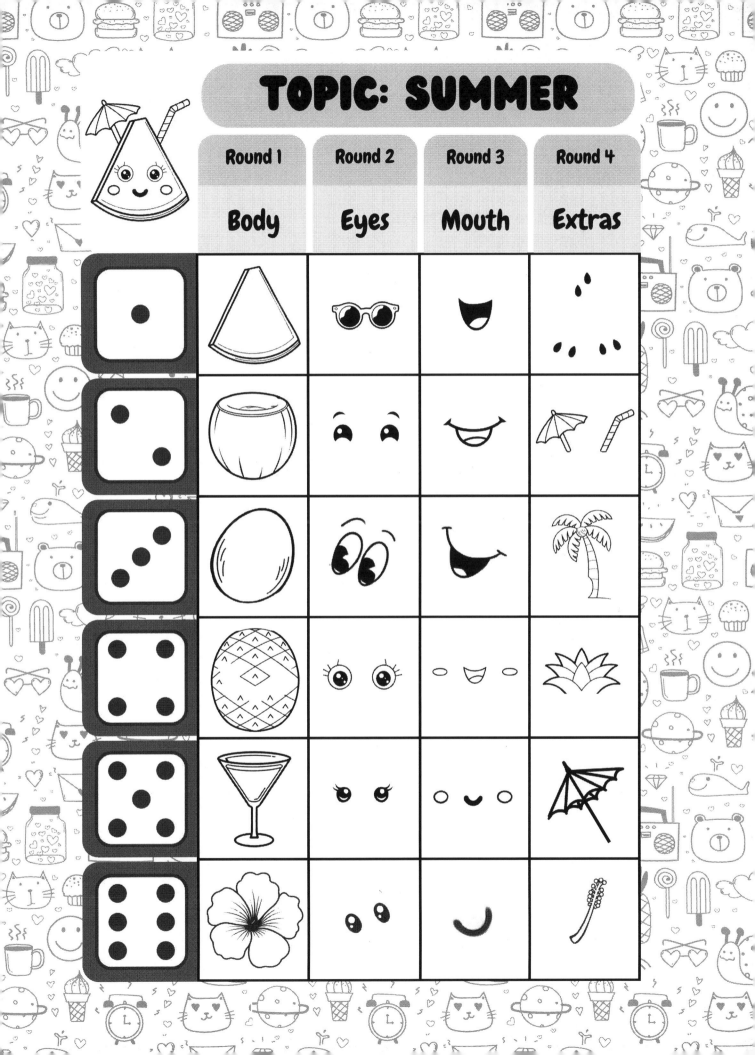

THIS IS WHAT YOU NEED FOR THIS LEVEL

TOPIC: FALL

Step 1

Step 2

Step 3

Step 4

Step 1

Step 2

Step 3

Step 4

TOPIC: FALL

Step 1

Step 2

Step 3

Step 4

Step 1

Step 2

Step 3

Step 4

TOPIC: FALL

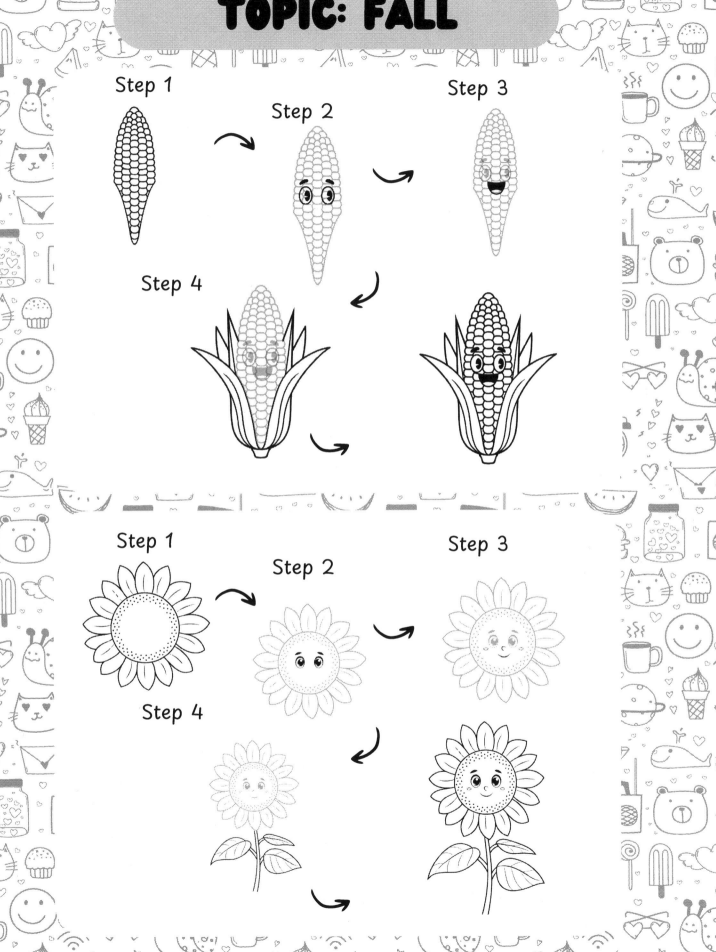

Step 1
Step 2
Step 3
Step 4

Step 1
Step 2
Step 3
Step 4

ROLL THE DICE AND BE SURPRISED

Here are a few silly combinations

TOPIC: FALL

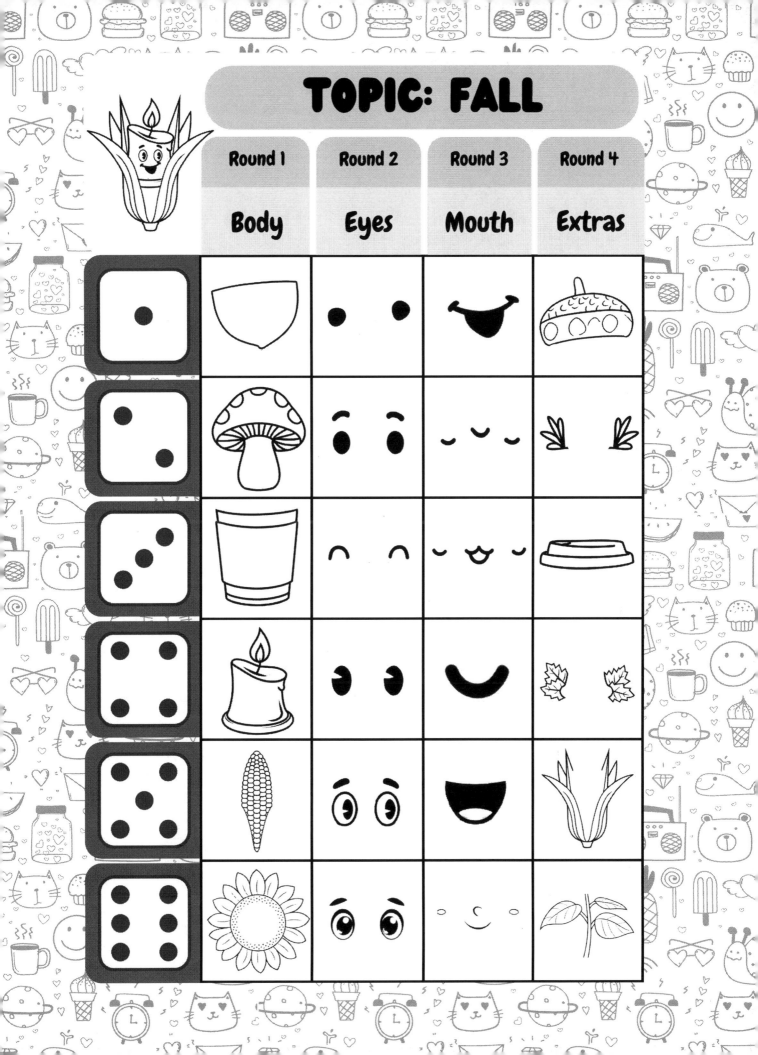

	Round 1 Body	Round 2 Eyes	Round 3 Mouth	Round 4 Extras

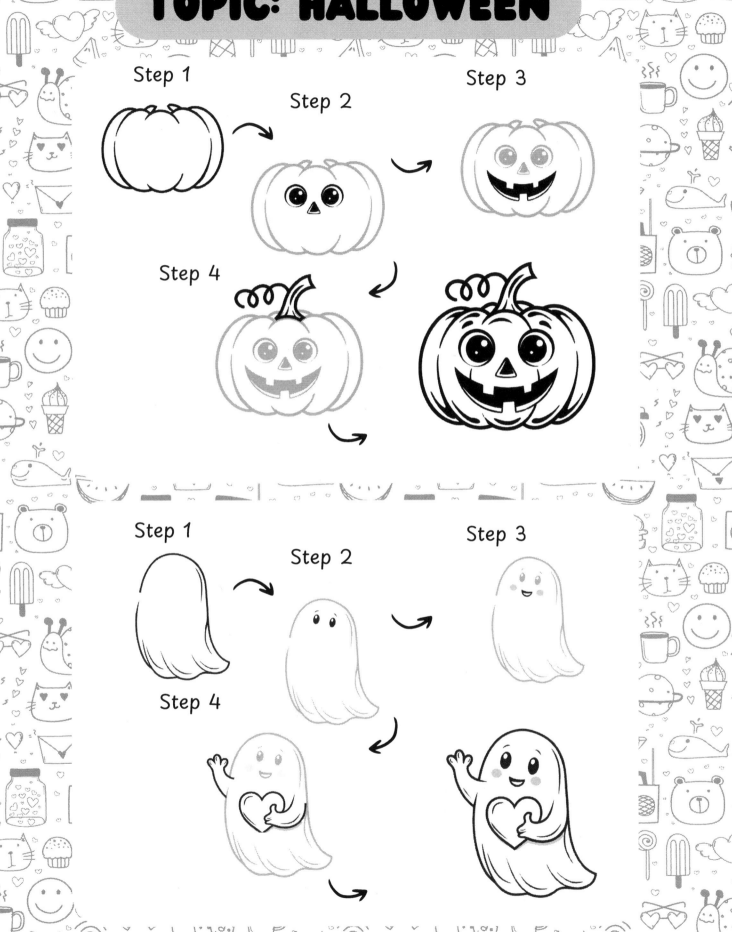

Step 1

Step 2

Step 3

Step 4

Step 1

Step 2

Step 3

Step 4

TOPIC: HALLOWEEN

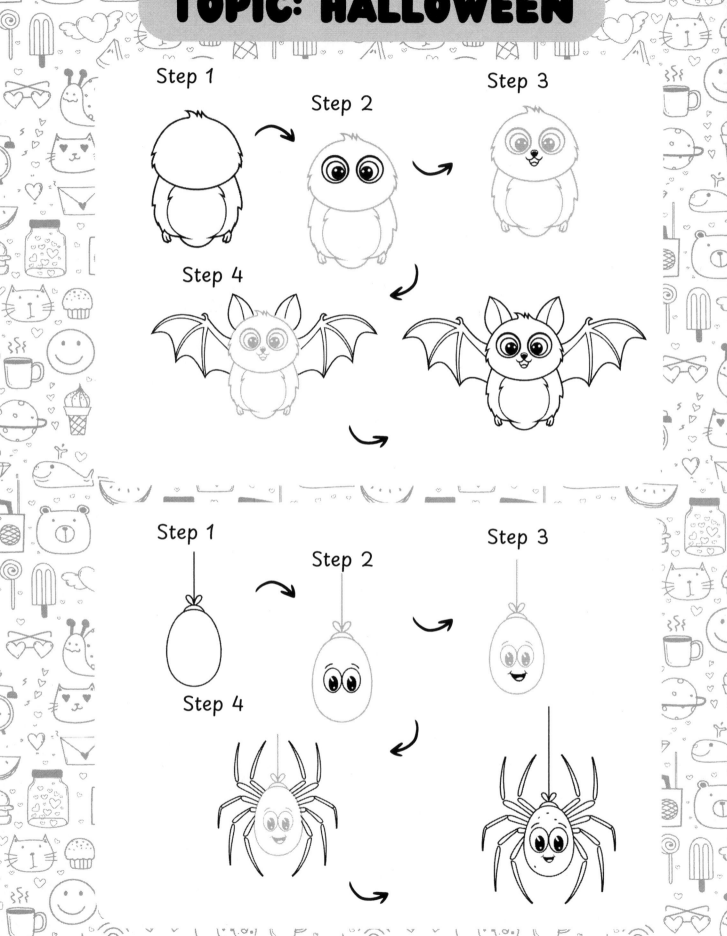

Step 1

Step 2

Step 3

Step 4

Step 1

Step 2

Step 3

Step 4

TOPIC: HALLOWEEN

Step 1

Step 2

Step 3

Step 4

Step 1

Step 2

Step 3

Step 4

ROLL THE DICE AND BE SURPRISED

Here are a few silly combinations

TOPIC: HALLOWEEN

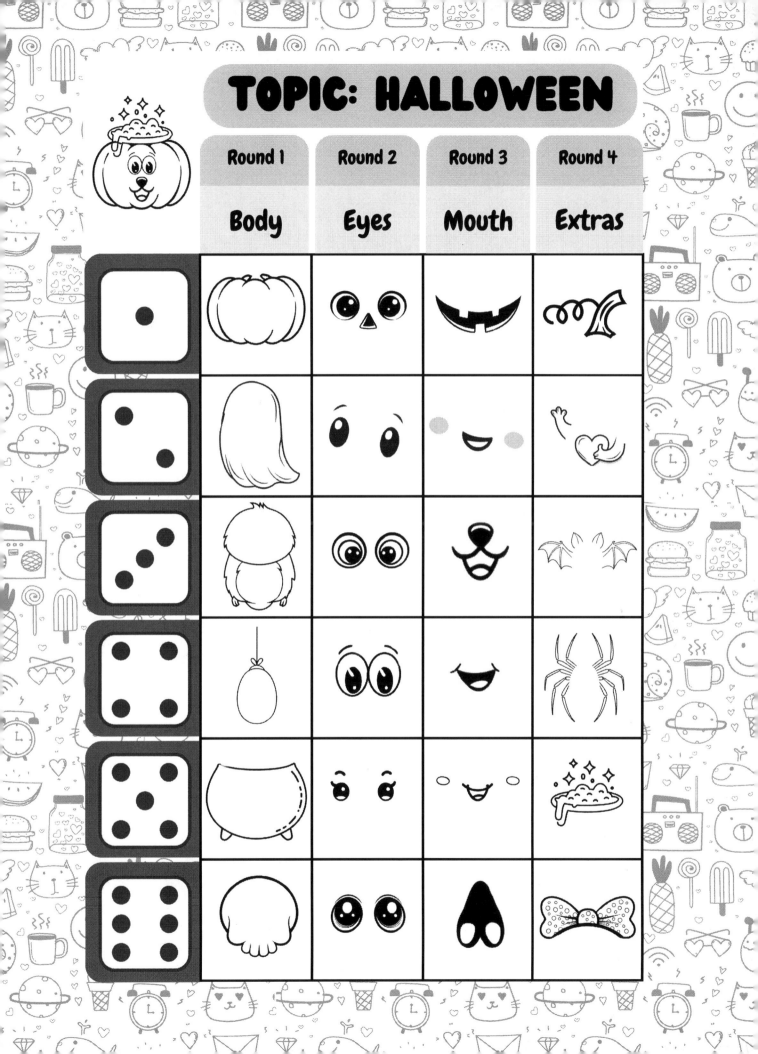

THIS IS WHAT YOU NEED FOR THIS LEVEL

TOPIC: CHRISTMAS

Step 1

Step 2

Step 3

Step 4

Step 1

Step 2

Step 3

Step 4

Step 1

Step 2

Step 3

Step 4

Step 1

Step 2

Step 3

Step 4

Step 1

Step 2

Step 3

Step 4

Step 1

Step 2

Step 3

Step 4

ROLL THE DICE AND BE SURPRISED

Here are a few silly combinations

TOPIC: CHRISTMAS

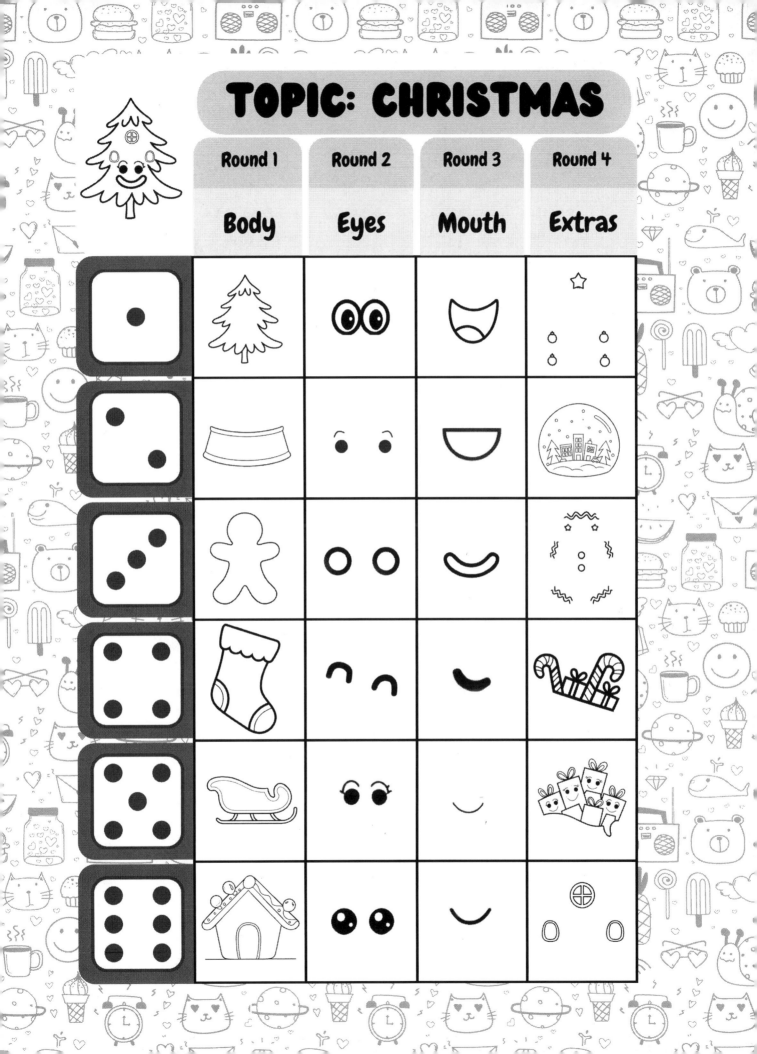

TOPIC: WINTER

Step 1

Step 2

Step 3

Step 4

Step 1

Step 2

Step 3

Step 4

TOPIC: WINTER

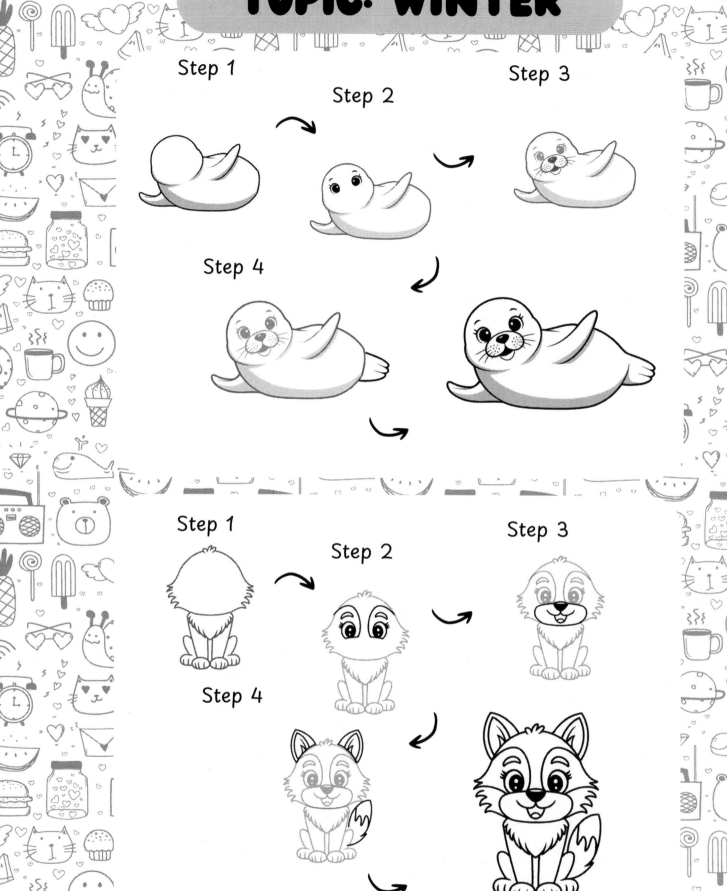

Step 1

Step 2

Step 3

Step 4

Step 1

Step 2

Step 3

Step 4

TOPIC: WINTER

Step 1   Step 2   Step 3

Step 4

Step 1   Step 2   Step 3

Step 4

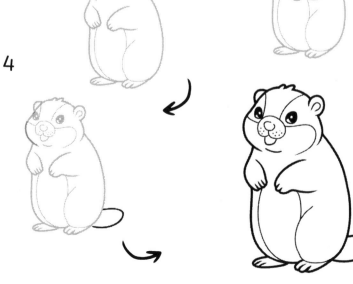

ROLL THE DICE AND BE SURPRISED

Here are a few silly combinations

TOPIC: WINTER

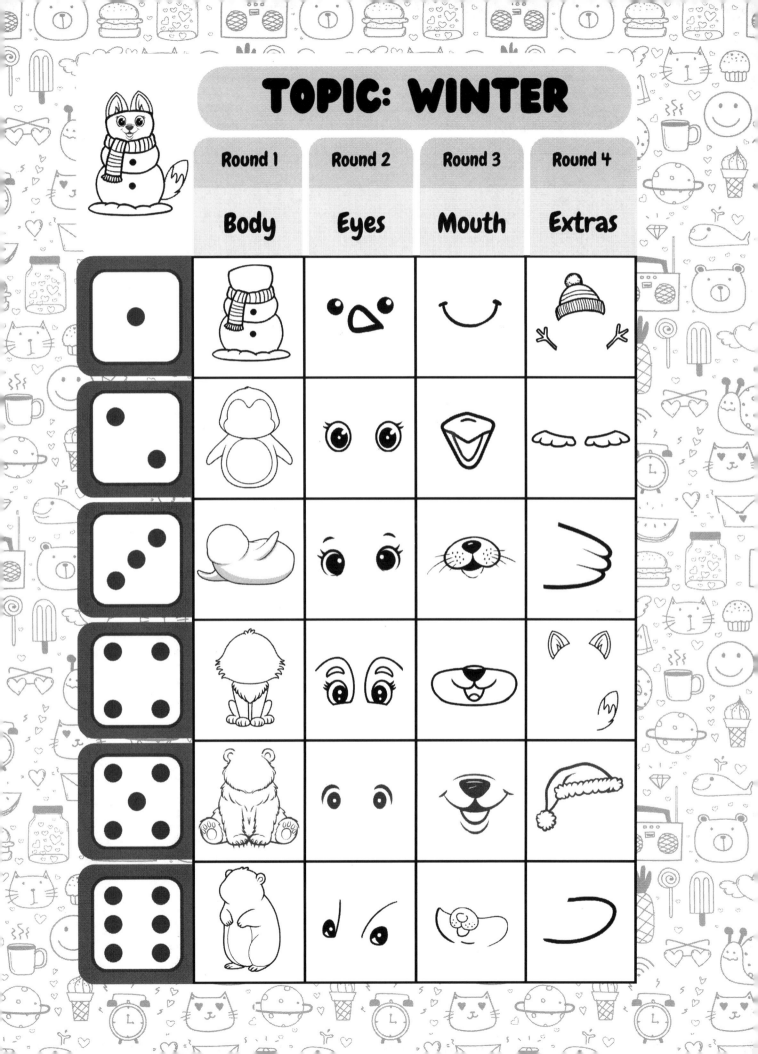

	Round 1 Body	Round 2 Eyes	Round 3 Mouth	Round 4 Extras

Download my Underwater Coloring Book and receive it for free straight to your email!

50 adorable sea-themed designs

Scan here or go to
geni.us/drawbook

TOPIC: SPACE

TOPIC: SPACE

Step 1

Step 2

Step 3

Step 4

Step 1

Step 2

Step 3

Step 4

TOPIC: SPACE

Step 1

Step 2

Step 3

Step 4

Step 1

Step 2

Step 3

Step 4

ROLL THE DICE AND BE SURPRISED

Here are a few silly combinations

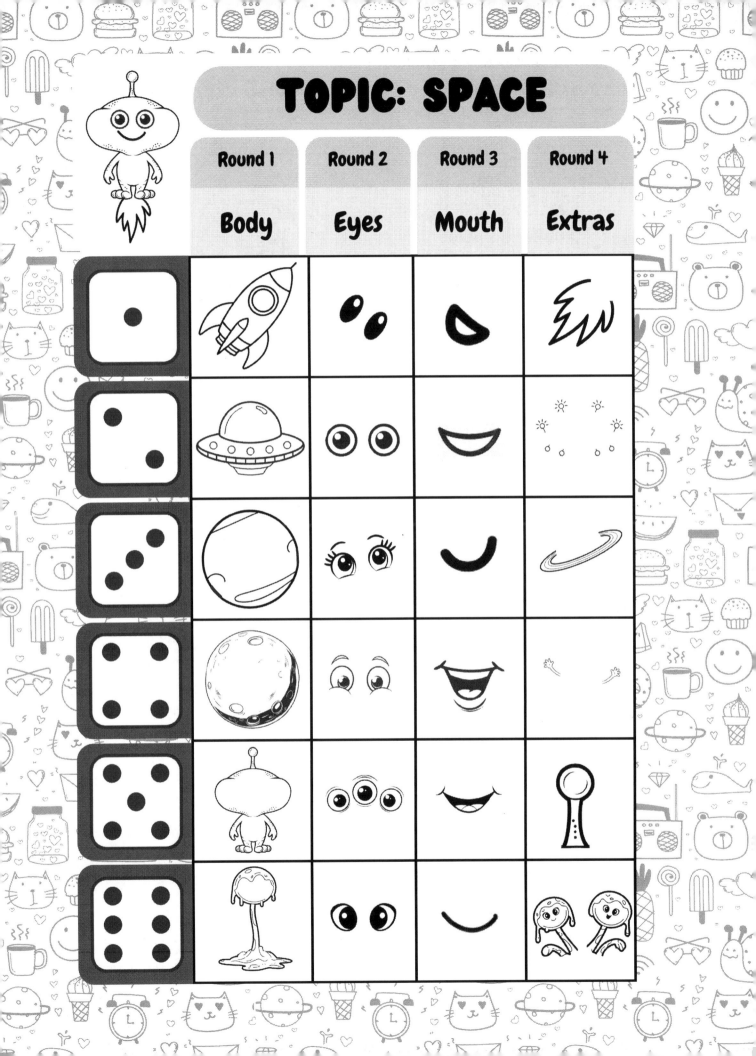

TOPIC: SPACE

	Round 1 **Body**	Round 2 **Eyes**	Round 3 **Mouth**	Round 4 **Extras**

TOPIC: FARM ANIMALS

Step 1

Step 2

Step 3

Step 4

Step 1

Step 2

Step 3

Step 4

Step 1

Step 2

Step 3

Step 4

Step 1

Step 2

Step 3

Step 4

TOPIC: FARM ANIMALS

Step 1

Step 2

Step 3

Step 4

Step 1

Step 2

Step 3

Step 4

ROLL THE DICE AND BE SURPRISED

Here are a few silly combinations

TOPIC: FARM ANIMALS

	Round 1 Body	Round 2 Eyes	Round 3 Mouth	Round 4 Extras
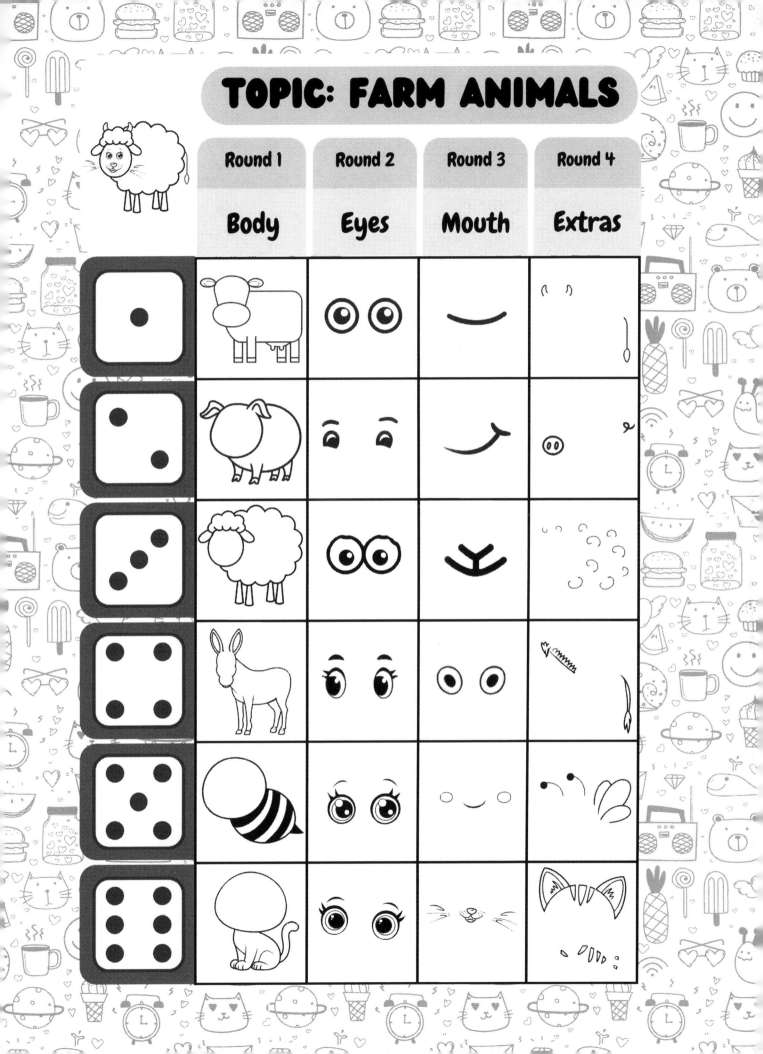

THIS IS WHAT YOU NEED FOR THIS LEVEL

TOPIC: UNDERWATER

Step 1

Step 2

Step 3

Step 4

Step 1

Step 2

Step 3

Step 4

TOPIC: UNDERWATER

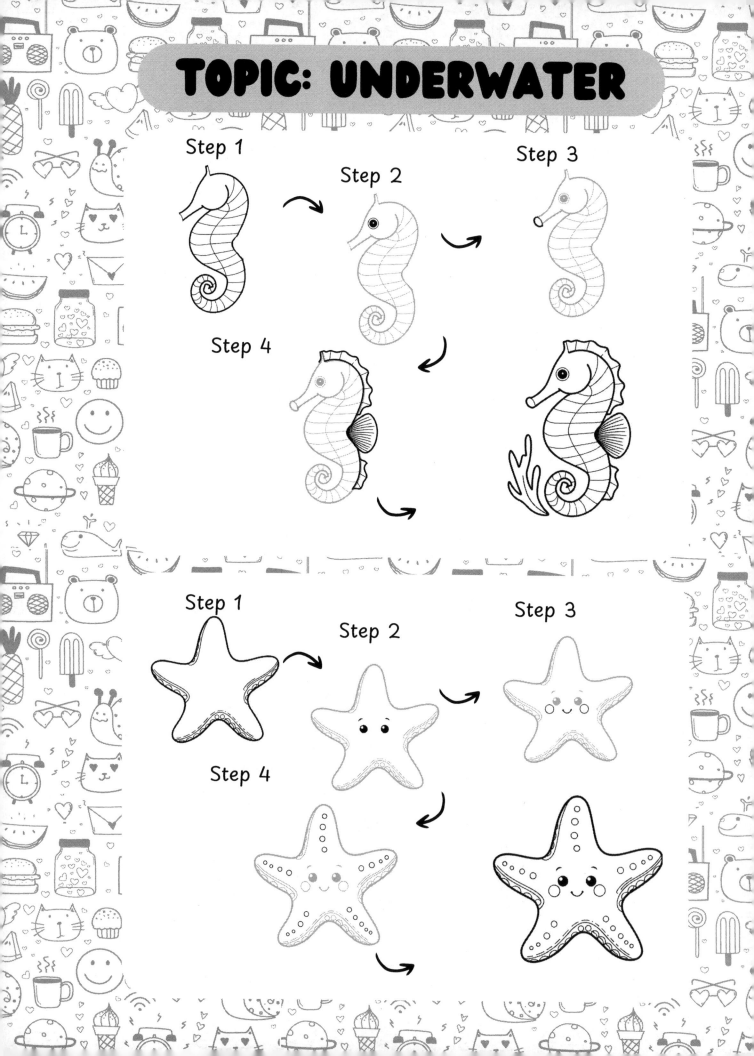

Step 1

Step 2

Step 3

Step 4

Step 1

Step 2

Step 3

Step 4

TOPIC: UNDERWATER

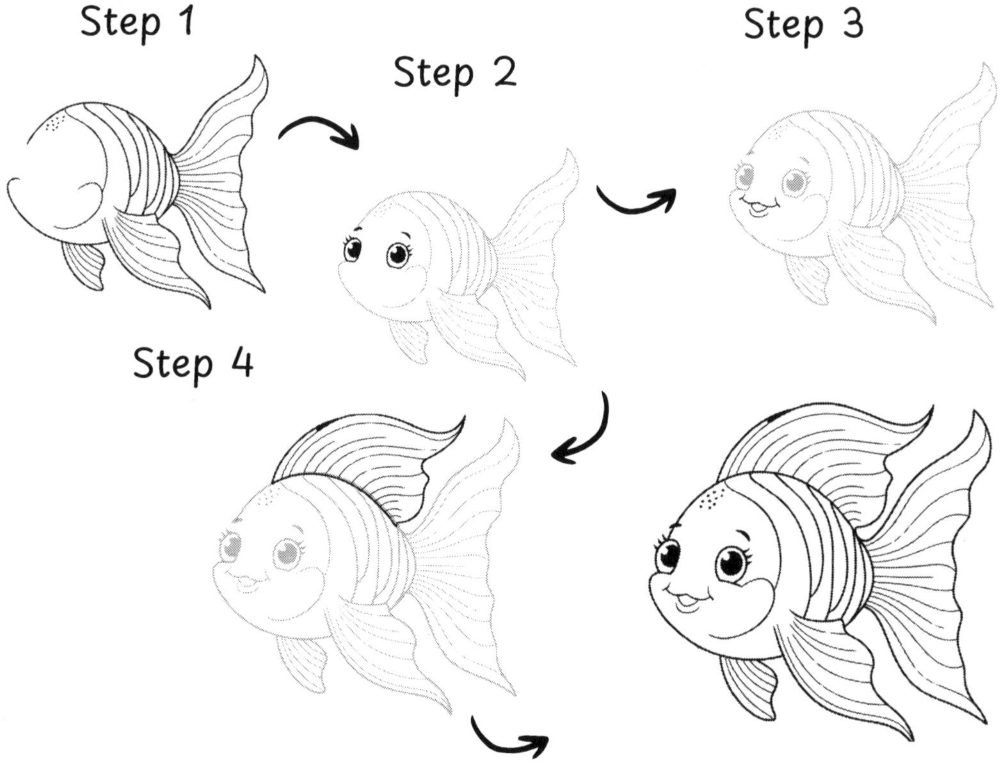

Step 1

Step 2

Step 3

Step 4

Step 1

Step 2

Step 3

Step 4

ROLL THE DICE AND BE SURPRISED

Here are a few silly combinations

TOPIC: UNDERWATER

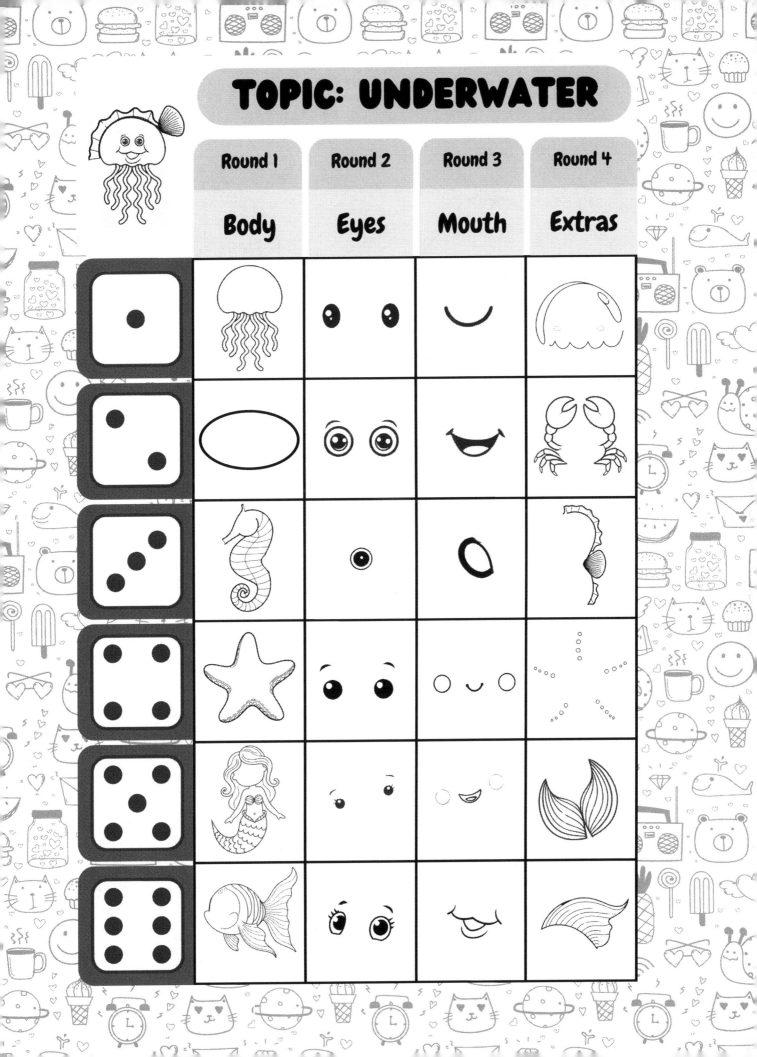

	Round 1 Body	Round 2 Eyes	Round 3 Mouth	Round 4 Extras

TOPIC: COZY

Step 1

Step 2

Step 3

Step 4

Step 1

Step 2

Step 3

Step 4

TOPIC: COZY

Step 1

Step 2

Step 3

Step 4

Step 1

Step 2

Step 3

Step 4

TOPIC: COZY

Step 1

Step 2

Step 3

Step 4

Step 1

Step 2

Step 3

Step 4

ROLL THE DICE AND BE SURPRISED

Here are a few silly combinations

TOPIC: COZY

	Round 1 Body	Round 2 Eyes	Round 3 Mouth	Round 4 Extras
⚀	sugar pot	eyes with lashes	smiling mouth	steam & ear
⚁	hot drink	round eyes	small smile	crescent
⚂	fire	curved eyes	open mouth	logs
⚃	yarn ball	dot eyes	half smile	hooks
⚄	beanie hat	worried eyes	open smile	pom-pom
⚅	scarf	dot eyes	curved smile	eyelashes

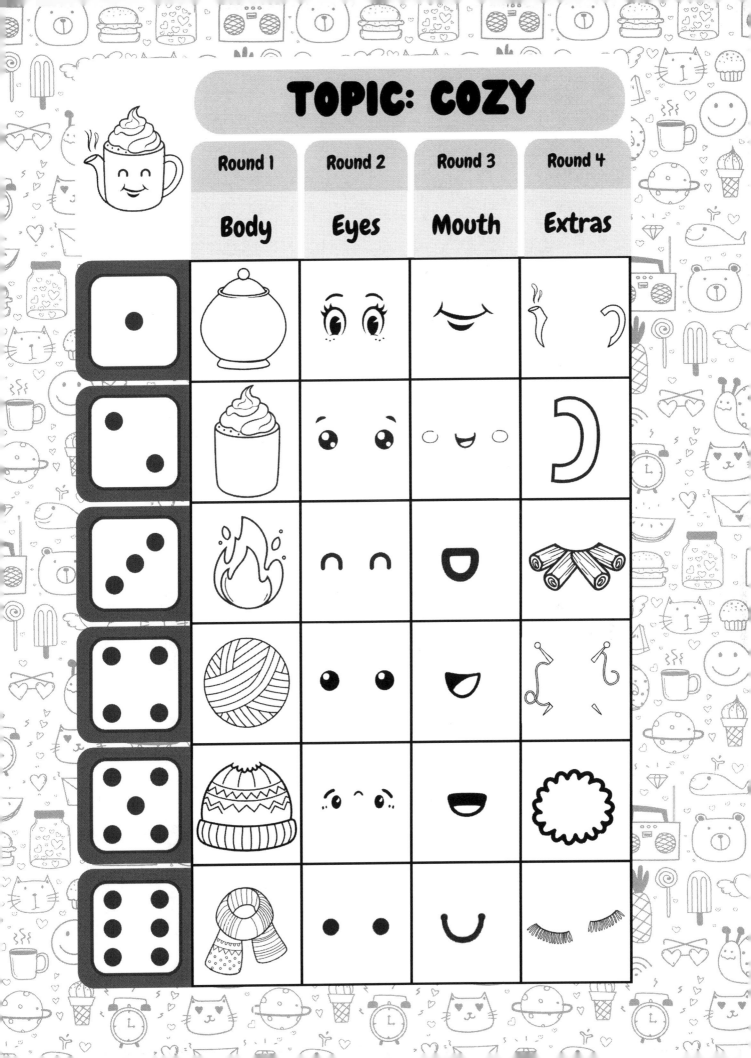

TOPIC: MAGIC

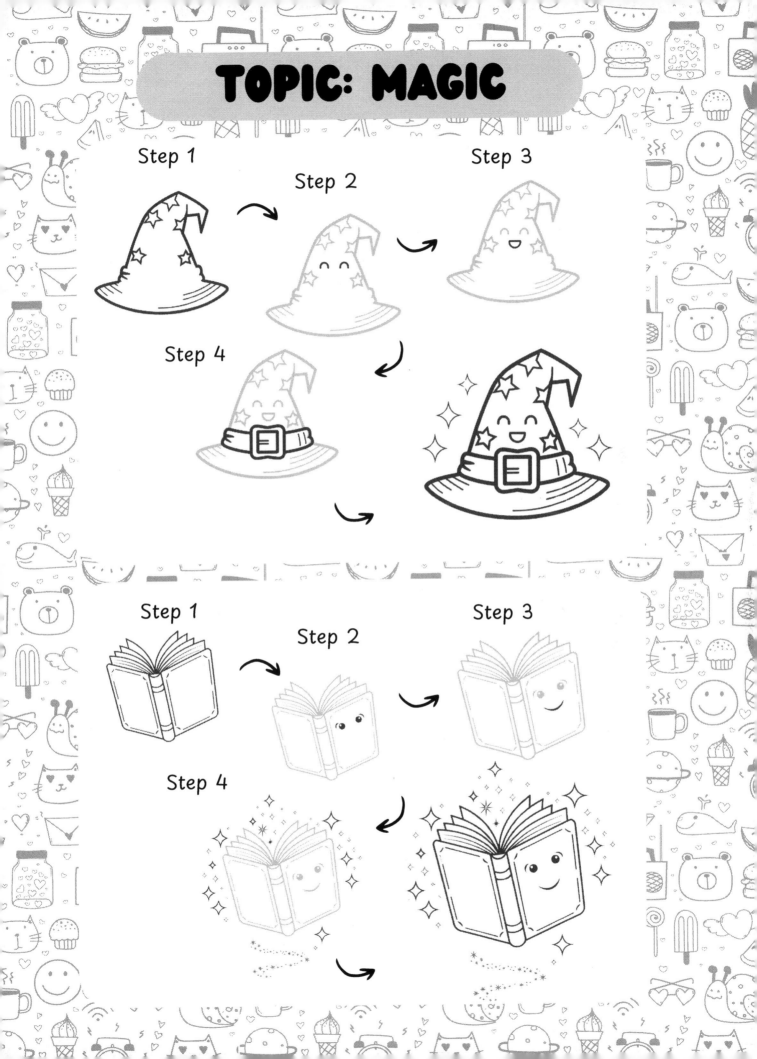

Step 1

Step 2

Step 3

Step 4

Step 1

Step 2

Step 3

Step 4

Step 1

Step 2

Step 3

Step 4

Step 1

Step 2

Step 3

Step 4

TOPIC: MAGIC

Step 1
Step 2
Step 3
Step 4

Step 1
Step 2
Step 3
Step 4

ROLL THE DICE AND BE SURPRISED

Here are a few silly combinations

TOPIC: MAGIC

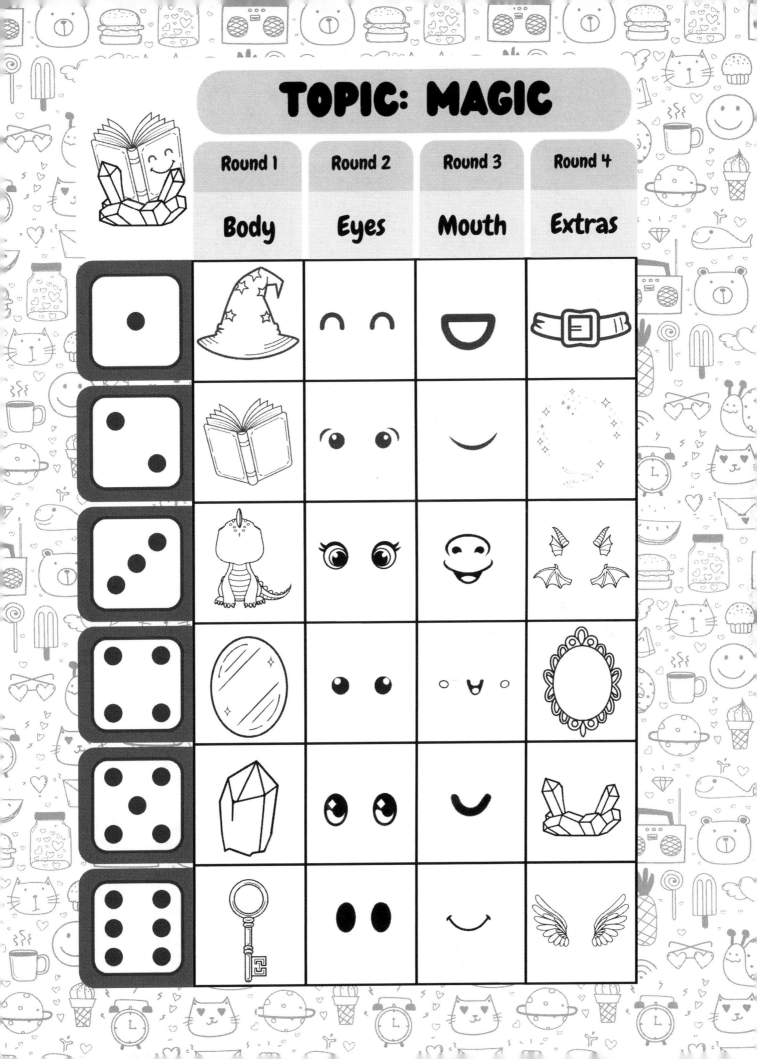

	Round 1 Body	Round 2 Eyes	Round 3 Mouth	Round 4 Extras
⚀	wizard hat			belt
⚁	book			sparkle circle
⚂	dragon			horns & wings
⚃	mirror			ornate mirror
⚄	crystal			crystals
⚅	key			wings

THIS IS WHAT YOU NEED FOR THIS LEVEL

TOPIC: PIRATES

Step 1

Step 2

Step 3

Step 4

Step 1

Step 2

Step 3

Step 4

TOPIC: PIRATES

Step 1

Step 2

Step 3

Step 4

Step 1

Step 2

Step 3

Step 4

TOPIC: PIRATES

Step 1

Step 2

Step 3

Step 4

Step 1

Step 2

Step 3

Step 4

ROLL THE DICE AND BE SURPRISED

Here are a few silly combinations

TOPIC: PIRATES

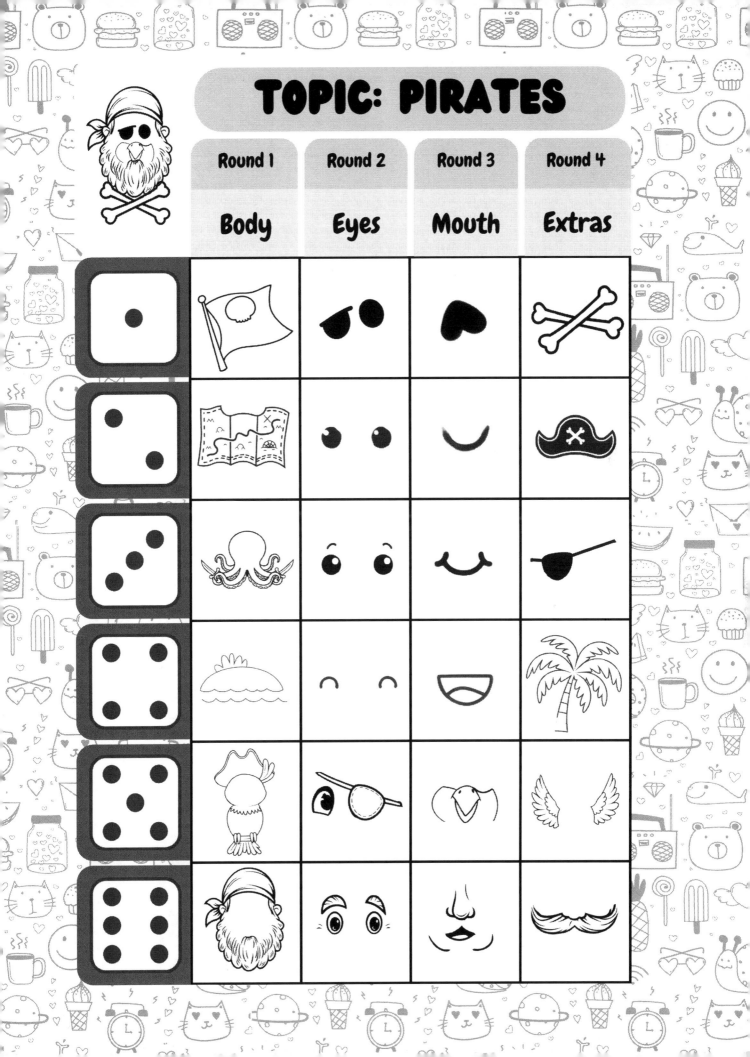

Made in the USA
Columbia, SC
12 November 2024

46312939R00052